SERMONS
—— in a ——
SENTENCE

SERMONS
—— in a ——
SENTENCE

Powerful Messages
in Five Words or Less

John Bytheway

DESERET
BOOK

Salt Lake City, Utah

Library of Congress Cataloging-in-Publication Data

Bytheway, John, 1962– author.
   Sermons in a sentence : powerful messages in five words or less / John Bytheway.
      pages cm
   Includes bibliographical references.
   Summary: Quotations from the Bible, the Book of Mormon, the Doctrine and Covenants, and the Pearl of Great Price, with brief commentary.
   ISBN 978-1-60907-167-7 (paperbound)
   1. Book of Mormon—Quotations. 2. Bible—Quotations.
3. Doctrine and Covenants—Quotations. 4. Pearl of Great Price—Quotations. 5. Church of Jesus Christ of Latter-day Saints—Doctrines. 6. Mormon Church—Doctrines. 7. Quotations, American. I. Title.
   BX8627.B98 2012
   289.3'2—dc23   2012023487

Printed in the United States of America
Malloy Lithographing Incorporated, Ann Arbor, MI

10   9   8   7   6   5

To Joseph Fielding McConkie

who changed my life in five words:

"We read scriptures too fast."

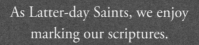

As Latter-day Saints, we enjoy
marking our scriptures.

Sometimes we mark entire verses.

Sometimes we mark sentences within a verse.

Sometimes we mark a single phrase.

*And sometimes, we find a sermon
in a single word.*

CONTENTS

WORDS

Repent (Matthew 4:17). 2

Remember (1 Nephi 10:20) 4

Endure (3 Nephi 15:9) 6

Stand (Ephesians 6:13) 8

Behold (Matthew 1:23). 10

Beware (D&C 38:39). 12

Go (Exodus 4:12). 14

Rejoice (2 Nephi 4:30) 16

Awake (2 Nephi 8:17) 18

TWO WORDS

I Am (Exodus 3:14). 22

Redemption Cometh (Mosiah 16:15). 24

Fear Not (Luke 2:10) 26

Infinite Atonement (2 Nephi 9:7) 28

Jesus Wept (John 11:35) 30

Tender Mercies (1 Nephi 1:20) 32

Without Spot (Moroni 10:33) 34

How Long? (Alma 14:26). 36

My Jesus (2 Nephi 33:6) 38

IN THREE WORDS

Favored of God (1 Nephi 17:35) 42

Towards the Temple (Mosiah 2:6) 44

Thou Shalt Love (Matthew 22:37–39) 46

Thou Art Able (Ether 3:5) 48

Not Knowing Beforehand (1 Nephi 4:6) 50

But If Not (Daniel 3:17–18) 52

My Soul Hungered (Enos 1:4) 54

Charity Never Faileth (1 Corinthians 13:8). . . 56

Continue to Minister (3 Nephi 18:32) 58

Man Is Nothing (Moses 1:10) 60

MESSAGES IN FOUR WORDS

We Believe in Being (Articles of Faith 1:13) . . 64

Wickedness Never Was Happiness

    (Alma 41:10). 66

Release Thyself from Bondage (D&C 19:35) . . 68

Hoisted upon Every Tower (Alma 46:36) 70

We Heeded Them Not (1 Nephi 8:33) 72

Bridle All Your Passions (Alma 38:12) 74

The Consequences of Sin (2 Nephi 9:48) 76

Thou Art Still Chosen (D&C 3:10). 78

Can Ye Look Up? (Alma 5:19) 80

POWERFUL MESSAGES IN FIVE WORDS

Let Him Ask of God (James 1:5) 84

Here Am I, Send Me (Abraham 3:27) 86

Art Thou Greater Than He? (D&C 122:8) . . . 88

Laboring with Their Own Hands

(Mosiah 27:4) 90

The Day of This Life (Alma 34:32) 92

Are We Not All Beggars? (Mosiah 4:19) 94

Pure Hearts and Clean Hands (2 Nephi 25:16) 96

Great Privilege of Our Church (Alma 61:14) . . 98

That I May Heal You (3 Nephi 9:13) 100

WORDS

REPENT

Repent: *for the kingdom of heaven is at hand.*

—Matthew 4:17

TO REPENT IS TO TURN, TO CHANGE, TO RE-EVALUATE, AND TO RECOMMIT. At times the word appears as a command, and at other times it invites with mercy and the promise of forgiveness. The word *repent* denotes sorrow and regret, but also peace and assurance. The fact that the word exists in scripture at all brings hope since without the possibility of repentance, all would be lost. Each time the Lord or His prophets command repentance, they are saying, "You have now been given another chance—another opportunity to change."

Elder D. Todd Christofferson taught: "Repentance is a divine gift, and there should be a smile on our faces when we speak of it. It points us to freedom, confidence, and peace. Rather than interrupting the celebration, the gift of repentance is the cause for true celebration" ("The Divine Gift of Repentance," *Ensign,* November 2011, 38).

REMEMBER

*Therefore **remember**, O man, for all thy doings thou shalt be brought into judgment.*

—1 Nephi 10:20

WATCH FOR THE WORD *REMEMBER* AS YOU READ THE SCRIPTURES, particularly the Book of Mormon. Also watch for its opposite, *forget*. Helaman pleads with his sons to "remember, remember . . ." (Helaman 5:12), while Captain Moroni questions Pahoran three times in one verse, "Have ye forgotten?" (Alma 60:20).

President Spencer W. Kimball taught, "When you look in the dictionary for the most important word, do you know what it is? It could be 'remember.' Because all of you have made covenants—you know what to do and you know how to do it—our greatest need is to remember. That is why everyone goes to sacrament meeting every Sabbath day, to take the sacrament and listen to the priests pray that they 'may always remember him and keep his commandments which he has given them.' Nobody should ever forget to go to sacrament meeting. 'Remember' is the word. 'Remember' is the program" ("Circles of Exaltation," address to Religious Educators, June 28, 1968, 8).

ENDURE

*Look unto me, and **endure** to the end, and ye shall live; for unto him that endureth to the end will I give eternal life.*

—3 Nephi 15:9

FOR MANY OF US, THE WORD *ENDURE* CONJURES UP FEELINGS OF PAIN OR FATIGUE, accompanied by images of weary saints doggedly staying the course amidst hardship. A friend said to me, "Most of those 'endure to the end' talks depress the dickens out of me." But endurance is not so much about pain as it is about resolution.

Stephen E. Robinson has written: "The critical question is not one of *getting into* the kingdom but of *staying* in the kingdom—of enduring to the end. For we must choose on an ongoing basis to remain, and that choice must be reflected in what we love and in what we seek. That is why enduring to the end is the fifth principle of the gospel. Daily, our question shouldn't be 'Have I made it to the kingdom yet?' but rather, 'Do I still want to stay?'" (*Following Christ* [1995], 17–18).

STAND

*Wherefore take unto you
the whole armour of God, that
ye may be able to withstand
in the evil day, and
having done all,
to **stand**.*

—Ephesians 6:13

WE USE THE WORD *STAND* AND MANY OF ITS FORMS IN OUR RELIGIOUS DISCOURSE: Stand, standards, take a stand, stand up for your beliefs, and stand for something or you'll fall for anything! To stand is to represent something, to stay in a fixed position, to be unmoved.

The opposite of standing is falling, buckling, wilting, or compromising. When Mike Wallace of *60 Minutes* asked President Gordon B. Hinckley how he accounted for the rapid growth of the Church, President Hinckley responded using the word *stand*, or a form thereof, three times: "We have standards that we expect them to live by and to uphold. It is demanding. And that is one of the things that attracts people to this Church. It stands as an anchor in a world of shifting values. They feel they have something solid that they are standing on while the ground is moving beneath them" (in Sheri L. Dew, *Go Forward with Faith* [1996], 540–41).

BEHOLD

Behold, *a virgin shall be with child, and shall bring forth a son, and they shall call his name Emmanuel, which being interpreted is, God with us.*

—Matthew 1:23

B*EHOLD* CAN BE DIVIDED INTO TWO WORDS, TO *BE* AND TO *HOLD*. More than just seeing something with our eyes, early definitions of the word *behold* meant "to keep hold of," or "to belong to." *Behold* is the word used by the Lord, by His angels, and by the authors of scripture who proclaim, "I want you to see this!" or, "I want you to hold onto it," or, "Look with your own eyes."

The word *behold* is a marker, a red flag, a flashing light within the scriptures that says, "Witness prophecy fulfilled." When we encounter *behold*, we know that something important or wonderful follows. "Behold, a marvelous work is about to come forth among the children of men" (D&C 4:1). "Behold the Lamb of God" (John 1:29). "Behold, the bridegroom cometh" (Matthew 25:6). See it, witness it, and hold onto it as a testimony.

BEWARE

Beware *of pride, lest ye become as the Nephites of old.*

—D&C 38:39

THE WORD *BEHOLD* AND ITS COMPANION *BEWARE* TEACH US WHAT TO LOOK AT—and what to look away from. *Behold* points us to the Lord's prophecies fulfilled, while *beware* urges us to "be wary" of Satan's traps and snares.

In our journeys through the scriptures, we encounter men and women of many kinds, some of whom are examples, and some of whom are warnings. We behold the examples; we hold on to what they did and to the principles they taught by their lives and their actions. But we beware of the warnings. We are encouraged to "be wary" of the temptations that seduced them, for the same temptations might also seduce us.

GO

*Therefore **go**, and I will be with thy mouth, and teach thee what thou shalt say.*

—Exodus 4:12

THERE IS A TIME TO PONDER, AND THERE IS A TIME TO PRODUCE. When Enoch complained that he was slow of speech, the Lord said, "Go forth and do as I have commanded thee . . ." (Moses 6:32). Isaiah admonished the house of Israel, "Go ye forth of Babylon" (Isaiah 48:20). Lehi encouraged Nephi, "Therefore go, my son, and thou shalt be favored" (1 Nephi 3:6). Jesus told the centurion, "Go thy way; and as thou hast believed, so be it done unto thee" (Matthew 8:13). The parable of the Good Samaritan concluded when Jesus told the lawyer, "Go, and do thou likewise" (Luke 10:37). The resurrected Christ told the Apostles, "Go ye therefore, and teach all nations" (Matthew 28:19).

The word *go* in these scriptures implies not only action but direction. When Jesus asked the Twelve, "Will ye also go away?" Peter answered, "Lord, to whom shall we go? thou hast the words of eternal life" (John 6:67–68).

REJOICE

Rejoice, *O my heart, and cry unto the Lord, and say: O Lord, I will praise thee forever; yea, my soul will* **rejoice** *in thee, my God, and the rock of my salvation.*

—2 Nephi 4:30

THE GOSPEL MESSAGE IS A MESSAGE OF JOY. THERE IS A GOD, HE IS A GOD OF LOVE, and we are His children. He wants to save us and give us all that He has. He wants maximum joy and happiness for all of us. When Korihor preached against the existence of God, the chief judge Giddonah demanded, "Why do ye teach this people that there shall be no Christ, to interrupt their rejoicings?" (Alma 30:22).

In other words, if there is no belief in Christ, there is no reason to rejoice. Jesus conquered death and hell and sin. He fixes broken things and broken hearts. Indeed, it's hard to have a negative attitude about anything—*anything*—when our lives are built on Christ. Our abiding testimony of the Savior gives us a reason to rejoice with no interruptions.

AWAKE

***Awake*, *awake*,** *stand up,*
O Jerusalem.

—2 Nephi 8:17

WE HAVE A TENDENCY TO SNOOZE WHEN WE SHOULD BE AWAKE. The scriptures are a wake-up call from God. Lehi told his sons to "awake" and "put on the armor of righteousness" (2 Nephi 1:23). King Benjamin pled with his people to "awake to a remembrance of the awful situation of those that have fallen into transgression" (Mosiah 2:40). Alma invited the Zoramites to "awake and arouse [their] faculties" (Alma 32:27) as he taught them how to plant Christ in their hearts. When God's children are sinning or simply not living up to their spiritual potential, prophets are sent to shake them into spiritual consciousness. Modern alarm clocks are equipped with a "snooze button," a built-in procrastination device that allows postponing the inevitable. The scriptures address "spiritual snoozing," a dangerous postponing of becoming fully awake until it is "everlastingly too late" (Helaman 13:38). President Ezra Taft Benson warned, "We must be shakened and awakened from a spiritual snooze" (*The Teachings of Ezra Taft Benson* [1988], 404).

TWO WORDS

I AM

And God said unto Moses,
***I AM** THAT **I AM**: and he said,*
Thus shalt thou say unto the
*children of Israel, **I AM***
hath sent me unto you.

—Exodus 3:14

O NLY TWO WORDS, BUT WOW, WHAT WORDS! *I AM.* I EXIST; I AM REAL. A message as well as a proper noun, "I am" is a simple but powerful name! Whenever the children of Israel pondered the God they worshiped, they remembered His name, "I am." Thousands of years later, He is still "I am." He has not changed His name to "I was," or "I used to be," but He is still, "I am."

Alert readers of the New Testament will notice Jesus using this name/phrase again and again in His teachings, further testifying of His own identity: "*I am* that bread of life" (John 6:48), "*I am* the good shepherd" (John 10:11), "*I am* the way, the truth, and the life" (John 14:6), and "Before Abraham was, *I am*" (John 8:58).

REDEMPTION COMETH

*Teach them that **redemption cometh** through Christ the Lord, who is the very Eternal Father. Amen.*

—Mosiah 16:15

ONLY TWO WORDS, A PROPHECY FULL OF HOPE. "Redemption cometh" is a promise that has been anticipated and relied on by God's children for millennia. Ancient prophets spoke before Jesus came. Many believed the hopeful words of Abinadi and others who prophesied that "redemption cometh"—a promise that everything that had been spoken about the coming Redeemer for four millennia would, one day, come to pass.

Redemption cometh from sin, redemption cometh from death, redemption cometh for the whole house of Israel. Today, modern prophets speak thousands of years after Jesus' atoning work was completed. Nevertheless, we often find ourselves wading through difficulty, trials, sin, and other stresses of earth life, all of which are covered by the Atonement. So, even in the latter days, the words *redemption cometh* bring peace, hope, and a promise of divine relief.

FEAR NOT

Fear not*: for, behold, I bring you good tidings of great joy, which shall be to all people.*

—Luke 2:10

ANGELS BRINGING MESSAGES FROM HEAVENLY REALMS OFTEN BEGIN with these two words, "Fear not." Why would that be? Our fears are at war with our faith, and sometimes our fears appear to be winning the battle.

President Boyd K. Packer taught: "This is a great time to live. When times are unsettled, when the dangers persist, the Lord pours out His blessings upon His church and kingdom. I have been associated now in the councils of the Church for upwards of thirty years. During that time I have seen, from the sidelines at least, many a crisis. Among the leaders I have at times seen great disappointment, some concern, maybe some anxiety. One thing I have never seen is fear. Fear is the antithesis of faith. In this Church and in this kingdom there is faith" (*Things of the Soul* [1996], 195).

INFINITE ATONEMENT

Wherefore, it must needs be an **infinite atonement**—*save it should be an* **infinite atonement** *this corruption could not put on incorruption.*

—2 Nephi 9:7

WE STRUGGLE TO FIND WORDS THAT CAN ADEQUATELY DESCRIBE THE ATONEMENT. Who can do it justice? Who can reduce something infinite into finite terms? Elder Tad R. Callister has written: "The word infinite, as used in this context, may refer to an atonement that simultaneously applies retroactively and prospectively, oblivious to constraints and measurements of time. It may refer to an atonement that applies to all God's creations, past, present, and future, and thus is infinite in its application, duration and effect" (*The Infinite Atonement* [2000], 59).

President Boyd K. Packer also commented on the Atonement's infinite application: "There is no habit, no addiction, no rebellion, no transgression, no apostasy, no crime exempted from the promise of complete forgiveness. That is the promise of the atonement of Christ" ("The Brilliant Morning of Forgiveness," *Ensign,* November 1995, 20).

JESUS WEPT

Jesus wept.

—John 11:35

LAZARUS DIED, AND JESUS WEPT. WHY? Jesus knew that He could restore the life of Lazarus, and He knew that the Resurrection would one day bring everyone back from the dead. Perhaps Jesus delayed coming immediately to Lazarus' side because He knew of the common belief that the spirit of a deceased person would linger near the body for three days. So it could be that Jesus purposely waited an extra day so that His miracle could not be denied. Nevertheless, during those four days, Jesus' friends were mourning with profound sadness. Even though He knew Lazarus would rise from the dead, He still felt the sorrow His friends felt, and it touched Him.

Elder Paul H. Dunn taught that Jesus' tears were not primarily because of the death of Lazarus. Rather, He "wept in pure compassion for the pain and lack of understanding of his two friends" ("'Because I Have a Father,'" *Ensign,* May 1979, 9).

TENDER
MERCIES

*But behold, I, Nephi, will show unto you that the **tender mercies** of the Lord are over all those whom he hath chosen, because of their faith, to make them mighty even unto the power of deliverance.*

—1 Nephi 1:20

Elder David A. Bednar brought the phrase "tender mercies" into the Church's consciousness in a classic talk he gave in the April 2005 general conference. Since then, testimonies have been borne from pulpits around the world testifying of the Lord's "tender mercies," evidences that the Lord loves us, cares for us, and arranges little intersections in our lives where divine providence appears in a moment of need: *What made you choose that hymn? How did you know I needed a call from you? Can you imagine if that flat tire had come two minutes earlier?* Each of us has experienced these divine gifts, and President Henry B. Eyring taught that the principal reason we are encouraged to keep journals is to document the hand of the Lord in our lives—or, in other words, to record the Lord's tender mercies (see "O Remember, Remember," *Ensign,* November 2007, 66–67). Recalling the Lord's tender mercies will increase our gratitude and our testimonies—and inevitably, as the hymn says, "it will surprise [us] what the Lord has done" ("Count Your Blessings," *Hymns*, no. 241).

WITHOUT
SPOT

*Then are ye sanctified in Christ by the grace of God, through the shedding of the blood of Christ, which is in the covenant of the Father unto the remission of your sins, that ye become holy, **without spot**.*

—Moroni 10:33

A SPOT IS A BLEMISH, A STAIN, OR A MARK THAT ISN'T SUPPOSED TO BE THERE. Throughout the Old Testament the children of Israel were commanded to offer up sacrifices using animals "without spot" (Numbers 28:3). Why? Because the animal sacrifices foreshadowed the sacrifice of Jesus, who was sinless and perfect and without spot. Happily, because Jesus shed His blood in Gethsemane and Golgotha, because of the miracle of the Atonement, we can also become clean and pure and without spot. The Apostle James taught that part of pure religion was to keep oneself "unspotted from the world" (James 1:27). Toward the end of Nephi's record, he mentioned that he would meet many souls at the judgment seat of Christ. But a closer reading reveals that Nephi was referring to more than just a nice heavenly reunion. Notice the extra word—Nephi hoped to meet "many souls *spotless* at his judgment-seat" (2 Nephi 33:7; emphasis added). Through Christ, we can become holy, without spot.

HOW LONG?

And Alma cried, saying:
How long *shall we suffer these*
great afflictions, O Lord?
O Lord, give us strength
according to our faith which is in
Christ, even unto deliverance.

—Alma 14:26

PART OF TRUSTING IN GOD IS TRUSTING IN HIS TIMING. Patience is hard. Waiting for the Lord to intervene can be excruciating. Job cried out "how long?" and so did David (see Job 7:19; Psalm 6:3). John the Revelator saw the martyrs throughout the ages who "cried with a loud voice, saying, How long, O Lord, holy and true, dost thou not judge and avenge our blood on them that dwell on the earth?" (Revelation 6:10). In our day, the Prophet Joseph Smith cried out from Liberty Jail, "How long shall thy hand be stayed," and, "How long shall they suffer these wrongs and unlawful oppressions . . . ?" (D&C 121:2–3). The Lord responds to all of these petitions, and to each of us who has ever asked the same question, out of His infinite perspective: "My son, peace be unto thy soul; thine adversity and thine afflictions shall be but a small moment" (D&C 121:7). Incredible as it may seem in the middle of our adversity, the Lord's promise is that one day, all of our current "how longs" will be remembered as "small moments."

MY JESUS

*I glory in plainness; I glory in truth; I glory in **my Jesus**, for he hath redeemed my soul from hell.*

—2 Nephi 33:6

WE ARE ACCUSTOMED TO SPEAKING OF OUR HEAVENLY FATHER and the Lord Jesus Christ in King James English. We pray in "thees," "thys," and "thous," scriptural pronouns that provide a bit of distance, a verbal reverence that is appropriate and comfortable. Perhaps this is why Nephi's intimate phrase *my Jesus* stands out. "My Jesus" appears only once in our entire standard works, from Nephi's closing testimony in the Book of Mormon. Yes, Jesus is Jehovah, the Holy One of Israel, the Great I AM, the God of Abraham, Isaac, and Jacob, the Father of heaven and earth, the Lord Jesus Christ, and the Lord God Omnipotent. But to Nephi in his later years, He was also "my Jesus." Nephi lost his father and was hated by his brothers, so for him, the Savior was both as infinite as the universe and as intimate as a friend. James Farrell has written, "[Jesus'] work on our behalf is at once infinite and infinitesimal; it is so big that he offers redemption to all, and yet so small that he offers redemption to *me*" (*Falling to Heaven* [2012], 53).

IN THREE WORDS

FAVORED
OF GOD

He that is righteous is
favored of God.

—1 Nephi 17:35

ONE DOESN'T GET VERY FAR INTO THE BOOK OF MORMON (1 Nephi 1:1), before encountering an interesting, often puzzling idea. Nephi says he was "highly favored" of the Lord. What? Does the Lord have favorites? The answer is "yes." But not in the way we normally understand the term. God does not choose arbitrarily who His favorites are. *We* do. It's a voluntary position.

Think of it this way: There are Nephites, Lamanites, Jaredites, and Mulekites, and there are also Favor-ites. Anyone can be a Favor-ite. *We* choose Favor-ite status; *we* choose to be recipients of God's favor. Nephi later explained to his brothers the process of becoming a "Favor-ite": "Behold, the Lord esteemeth all flesh in one; he that is righteous is favored of God" (1 Nephi 17:35). We choose to be favored when we choose to be obedient. Does God love all of His children? Of course He does. But He is able to do more for those who honor Him and strive to serve Him (see D&C 130:21).

TOWARDS
THE TEMPLE

Every man having his tent with the door thereof ***towards the temple*** . . .

—Mosiah 2:6

King Benjamin couldn't address his people within the walls of the temple; his audience was too large. So he had a tower built near the grounds, and the people pitched their tents "towards the temple," where they could sit inside and listen. Where we choose to "pitch our tent" is a metaphor for our personal priorities. By contrast, Abraham's nephew Lot "dwelled in the cities of the plain, and pitched his tent toward Sodom. But the men of Sodom were wicked and sinners before the Lord exceedingly" (Genesis 13:12–13). These verses compel us to ask, "Where is my tent pitched— toward the temple, facing the world, or somewhere in between?" The world would like us to pitch our tents timidly and temporarily so that we can shift their orientation according to social pressure, the media, and our moods. But the gospel says, Make up your mind! Drive your stakes deep into the earth, determined to keep your heart, might, mind, and strength towards the Lord, His gospel, and His house.

THOU SHALT LOVE

Thou shalt love the Lord thy God with all thy heart, and with all thy soul, and with all thy mind. This is the first and great commandment. And the second is like unto it, **Thou shalt love** thy neighbour as thyself.

—Matthew 22:37–39

LEARNED MEN IN JESUS' DAY WOULD OFTEN WRESTLE with which of the 613 commandments in the books of Moses were the most important. When Jesus came along, the Pharisees asked for His opinion. Jesus answered that to love God and to love your neighbor encompassed and embraced all of the law and all of the other commandments. Notice that the two most important commandments both begin with the same three words, "Thou shalt love."

In the end, what we have learned from books, how many scriptures we've memorized, how many years of service we've acquired, or how many callings we've completed will be secondary to how much we have loved. As if to reinforce the point, Jesus, in the gospel of John, gave the key to identifying a true disciple of Christ: "By this shall all men know that ye are my disciples, if ye have love one to another" (John 13:35).

THOU
ART ABLE

Behold, O Lord, thou canst do this.
We know that **thou art able**
to show forth great power,
which looks small unto the
understanding of men.

—Ether 3:5

SCRIPTURALLY SPEAKING, ONLY GOD IS "ABLE." The best God's children can do is be "willing." In the hymn "Guide Us, O Thou Great Jehovah" (*Hymns*, no. 83), we sing, "We are weak, but thou art able." Indeed. In outlining the covenants we make to God as we partake of the sacrament, the prayers do not say, "And witness unto thee, O God, the Eternal Father, that they are *able* to take upon them the name of thy Son," but rather, "that they are *willing* . . ."

Since we cannot save ourselves or forgive ourselves, the best we can do is have a willing heart and rely on someone else who is able to save and forgive. The Lord said to Moses, "This is my work and my glory—to bring to pass the immortality and eternal life of man" (Moses 1:39), and we are wonderfully reassured that He later declared, "I am able to do mine own work" (2 Nephi 27:21).

NOT KNOWING
BEFOREHAND

And I was led by the Spirit,
not knowing beforehand *the*
things which I should do.

—1 Nephi 4:6

MOST OF US HAVE WILLING HEARTS AND HONEST DESIRES TO DO THE LORD'S WILL. The only problem is, much of the time we're not sure we know what the Lord's will is! So what do we do when we *don't* know what to do? That's the test. Nephi was given the task of getting the brass plates from Laban, but the Lord didn't tell him how to do it. Nephi and his brothers failed miserably in their first two attempts, resulting in the loss of the family treasure and nearly in the loss of their lives. After these setbacks, Nephi could have dropped to his knees with the thought, "I'm not going to stop praying until the Lord tells me exactly what to do." But very often, the Lord is silent in such a request, waiting until we act, or move forward in faith, before giving us what we need—not beforehand—but "in the very moment" when we need it (D&C 100:6). As President Marion G. Romney said, God "can only guide our footsteps when we move our feet" ("The Basic Principles of Church Welfare," *Ensign*, May 1981, 91).

BUT IF NOT

Our God whom we serve is able to deliver us from the burning fiery furnace, and he will deliver us out of thine hand, O king. **But if not***, be it known unto thee, O king, that we will not serve thy gods, nor worship the golden image which thou hast set up.*

—Daniel 3:17–18

SHADRACH, MESHACH, AND ABED-NEGO FACED A FIERY EXECUTION for refusing to worship idols. They knew that God could deliver them, but would He? Either way, these brave young men determined they would not worship a false god. As a consequence, they were thrown into a fiery furnace. But miraculously, they were not harmed. The Lord intervened! However, as the scriptures and our life experiences reveal, sometimes the Lord does *not* intervene. Sometimes the seagulls don't come, the mysterious envelope containing "just enough" doesn't arrive, and the sick are not healed. Then what? Yes, Shadrach, Meshach, and Abed-nego were saved, but Abinadi burned (see Mosiah 17:13). However, Abinadi's last words were not a complaint of being forsaken, but an expression of hope: "O God, receive my soul" (Mosiah 17:19). Our hope is that the Lord will intervene in our lives, *but if not*, we will discover whether our faith is real, or only something we hold onto when it appears to be working for our benefit.

MY SOUL HUNGERED

*And **my soul hungered;**
and I kneeled down
before my Maker.*

—Enos 1:4

THE STORY OF ENOS IS AS BRIEF AS IT IS PROFOUND. When his body hungered, he stood up on his feet and went hunting. When his soul hungered, he got down on his knees and prayed.

"Soul hunger" is more difficult to satisfy than physical hunger, but food for the soul has eternal staying power. The bread and water of the sacrament are emblems of the Atonement, specifically blessed "to the souls of all those who partake" of them (Moroni 4:3). Jesus, who called Himself the "bread of life," promised, "He that eateth of this bread shall live for ever" (John 6:35, 58). In the Sermon on the Mount, Jesus assured, "Blessed are they which hunger and thirst after righteousness" (Matthew 5:6). He might have said, "Blessed are the righteous," except that perfect righteousness is impossible for us to attain without Jesus. Thus, although we can eat to satisfy our bodies, Jesus is the sole provider of nourishment for the soul, leaving us, like Enos, to hunger and thirst after righteousness—which hunger, the Savior promised, shall be filled (see Matthew 5:6).

CHARITY NEVER FAILETH

Charity never faileth.

—1 Corinthians 13:8

IT'S THRILLING WHEN SCRIPTURES USE STRONG WORDS LIKE *NEVER, ALWAYS, FIRST, LAST,* AND *BEST*. Imagine how much weaker this phrase would be if it read, "Charity hardly ever faileth," or "There's a really good chance charity won't fail." Elder Bruce R. McConkie used strong words like *most* and *above all* when he commented on this verse: "Above all the attributes of godliness and perfection, charity is the one most devoutly to be desired. Charity is more than love, far more; it is everlasting love, perfect love, the pure love of Christ which endureth forever" (*Doctrinal New Testament Commentary,* 3 vols. [1965–73], 2:378). Since charity *never* fails, we should *always* strive to have it. President Thomas S. Monson used strong words like *everything* and *all* when he taught, "May this long enduring . . . motto, this timeless truth, guide you in everything you do. May it permeate your very souls and find expression in all your thoughts and actions" ("Charity Never Faileth," *Ensign,* November 2010, 125).

CONTINUE TO MINISTER

Nevertheless, ye shall not cast him out of your synagogues, or your places of worship, for unto such shall ye **continue to minister***; for ye know not but what they will return and repent.*

—3 Nephi 18:32

THE LORD NEVER GIVES UP ON ANYONE, AND NEITHER SHOULD WE. The Perfection First Ward in the Perfection Stake has yet to be created. Each of us stumbles through life, acquiring scars and, regrettably, causing a few. What do we do when someone falls away? We *continue* to *minister*. But what if people don't want to be ministered to?

Elder Von G. Keetch taught that by the time search-and-rescue crews reach victims on the mountain, they often don't want to be rescued. Typically, they finally feel warm and comfortable as a result of hypothermia. The rescuer knows what he must do: First, get the victims to trust him; second, give them something to do that will help them feel needed (such as calling home); and third, raise their body temperature with some warm nourishment. Similarly, for those who may not want to be rescued spiritually, we give them a friend, a responsibility, and some nourishment by the good word—we continue to minister.

MAN IS NOTHING

Now, for this cause I know that **man is nothing**, *which thing I never had supposed.*

—Moses 1:10

I SUSPECT THE PHRASE *MAN IS NOTHING* HAS NEVER BEEN USED AS A THEME for a youth conference. Yet that's exactly what is taught in Helaman 12:7: "O how great is the nothingness of the children of men; yea, even they are less than the dust of the earth." I must admit I enjoy watching my students struggle with this paradox in Book of Mormon class. They're used to hearing phrases like, "You've been saved for the last days," and, "You are a chosen generation." When they stumble upon a scripture that teaches "man is nothing," they ask, "Which is it? We're the best or we're the dust?" Both are true, but a little clearer when we add two clarifying words: Man is nothing *without God.* And yes, we're less than the dust when we ignore God's counsel, because dust obeys, and ofttimes we rebel (see Helaman 12:8). Moses understood his own nothingness but also his "somethingness," and he held these two ideas in perfect harmony. Almost immediately after he concluded "man is nothing," he countered Satan's temptation with a sort of divine self-concept, "Behold, I am a son of God" (Moses 1:13).

MESSAGES IN FOUR WORDS

WE BELIEVE IN BEING

We believe in being *honest, true, chaste, benevolent, virtuous, and in doing good to all men . . .*

—Articles of Faith 1:13

WHEN THE PROPHET JOSEPH SMITH ANSWERED THE QUERY of John Wentworth, the last paragraph he penned was the thirteenth article of faith. He could have written the first sentence in that closing paragraph as follows, "We believe in honesty, truth, chastity, benevolence and virtue. . . ." However, the gospel isn't just a set of beliefs; it's a formula for *becoming*. Thus, he inserted the clarifying word, "We believe in *being* . . ." More than just affirming widely accepted character traits like honesty and benevolence, we believe in *being*—or in other words, in becoming what we say we believe. Thus, the Articles of Faith should be a practice, not just a belief; a way of life, not just a way of thinking. Some have suggested that the thirteenth article of faith is merely a list of ethics, but that's why it's the thirteenth and not the first. The thirteenth article of faith is about becoming what obedience to the doctrines in articles of faith one through twelve will help us become—followers of the Lord Jesus Christ who rely on His Atonement and in the gospel He taught.

WICKEDNESS NEVER WAS HAPPINESS

Do not suppose, because it has been spoken concerning restoration, that ye shall be restored from sin to happiness. Behold, I say unto you, **wickedness never was happiness**.

—Alma 41:10

CORIANTON'S MISUNDERSTANDING OF THE WORD *RESTORATION* gave us perhaps the most widely known and oft-quoted phrase of Alma: a four-word sermon on behavior and consequences with mathematic precision. You cannot do wrong and feel right!

Samuel the Lamanite warned the Nephites of the futility of their behavior with similar clarity when he observed, "Ye have sought for happiness in doing iniquity . . ." (Helaman 13:38). Some may object and suggest that the wicked appear to be plenty happy. Malachi repeated the complaint of some who concluded that it was vain to serve God: "Now we call the proud happy; yea, they that work wickedness are set up; yea, they that tempt God are even delivered" (Malachi 3:15). But their "happiness" isn't lasting—it's temporary. As Jesus said, "they have joy in their works *for a season,* and by and by the end cometh" (3 Nephi 27:11; emphasis added). If it is really true that wickedness never was happiness, then the reverse is also true—righteousness always was.

RELEASE THYSELF FROM BONDAGE

Pay the debt thou hast contracted with the printer. **Release thyself from bondage**.

—D&C 19:35

HERE, THE SAVIOR OF THE WORLD GIVES A BRIEF COMMENT on personal finance. Jesus conquered the bondage of death, hell, and sin, but financial bondage is generally self-imposed, and therefore, the debtors hold the key to their own release! While the world was still reeling from the effects of the Great Depression, President J. Reuben Clark Jr. spoke on the bondage of debt and the interest that causes debt to grow: "Interest never sleeps nor sickens nor dies; it never goes to the hospital; it works on Sundays and holidays; it never takes a vacation. . . . Once in debt, interest is your companion every minute of the day and night; . . . and whenever you get in its way or cross its course or fail to meet its demands, it crushes you" (in Conference Report, April 1938, 103). Although the debt referred to in this verse of scripture was incurred for the noblest of purposes (for the printing of the Book of Mormon), the Lord Jesus Christ, who is the champion of agency and freedom, encouraged Martin Harris to eliminate the bondage of debt as swiftly as possible.

HOISTED UPON EVERY TOWER

And it came to pass also, that he caused the title of liberty to be **hoisted upon every tower** *which was in all the land, which was possessed by the Nephites; and thus Moroni planted the standard of liberty among the Nephites.*

—Alma 46:36

SOME OF US STRUGGLE TO FIND MEANING IN THE "WAR CHAPTERS" of the Book of Mormon. But every chapter contains spiritual gems like this one! After Captain Moroni wrote the title of liberty on his coat and caused the people to receive it by covenant, he hoisted it upon *every* tower. Towers served, among other things, as the media of ancient peoples, and we can only imagine how different our world would be today if the media reminded us to keep our covenants rather than abandon them. Moroni's enemy also used his towers to communicate. You'll notice that once Amalickiah achieved his designs, the first thing he did was "appoint men to speak unto the Lamanites from their towers, against the Nephites" (Alma 48:1).

Just as Moroni placed reminders of the covenant everywhere, we can do the same thing. We can display pictures of the Savior, the temple, and other scriptural heroes and spiritual reminders on our walls and in our rooms to remind us of covenants made in our hearts.

WE HEEDED
THEM NOT

And great was the multitude that did enter into that strange building. And after they did enter into that building they did point the finger of scorn at me and those that were partaking of the fruit also; but **we heeded them not**.

—1 Nephi 8:33

HEED IS A WORD RARELY USED IN MODERN CONVERSATION. We prefer *pay attention*. In Lehi's dream, the path was straight, but not without distraction and difficulty. Upon reaching the tree and tasting the exquisite fruit, spiritual travelers were assailed by the taunts and jeers of the occupants of the great and spacious building. In such a large structure, it's odd that the activity of choice was to stand on the porches and mock. Unfortunately, some of those who were partaking of the fruit were so affected by the ridicule that they wandered away and lost everything.

We may well ask ourselves, "To what or to whom do we give heed?" The scriptures warn us to "give heed to the words of the prophets and apostles" or be cut off (D&C 1:14). The consequences of paying heed to the great and spacious are chilling: "For as many as heeded them, had fallen away" (1 Nephi 8:34). Jesus modeled the ideal, because He "suffered temptations but gave no heed unto them" (D&C 20:22).

BRIDLE ALL YOUR PASSIONS

*Use boldness, but not overbearance; and also see that ye **bridle all your passions**, that ye may be filled with love; see that ye refrain from idleness.*

—Alma 38:12

"IF IT FEELS GOOD, DO IT" WAS THE MOTTO OF THE SIXTIES, and similar adaptations abound today. Some feel that they have the right to give in to every passion they have, and that not to do so would be repressive. "God gave me these feelings," the argument goes, "so why shouldn't I give them full expression?" On the other extreme is the notion that we should destroy or eliminate our passions altogether. But that is not what God is asking us to do. The key word here is *bridle*. A bridle is used on a horse not because the horse is bad, but because it is incredibly powerful, and its power must be controlled and directed. Bruce and Marie Hafen have written, "We restrain our passions and seek virtue not because romantic love is bad, but precisely because it is so good. It is not only good; it is pure, precious, even sacred and holy" ("'Bridle All Your Passions,'" *Ensign,* February 1994, 15). Immediately following Alma's counsel to "bridle" is the promise of being "filled with love." Interestingly, it is by reigning in our passions, not giving in to them, that we find a fulness of love.

THE CONSEQUENCES OF SIN

Behold, if ye were holy I would speak unto you of holiness; but as ye are not holy, and ye look upon me as a teacher, it must needs be expedient that I teach you **the consequences of sin**.

—2 Nephi 9:48

NEPHI'S BROTHER JACOB CHOSE TO TEACH NOT ONLY ABOUT SIN, the commandments, and the "dos and don'ts" of the gospel message, but about the consequences that follow. Focusing on consequences rather than actions alone is a brilliant teaching tool that allows listeners to draw conclusions from their own experience and from witnessing the experience of others. Pondering results of our actions gets us out of our short-term, "what do I want right now" mind-set. Once we are in a more forward-thinking mode, we can discern for ourselves that the short-term pleasure of sin is not worth the long-term pain that follows. Sister Sheri Dew used the consequences approach when she observed, "I have never known anyone who was happier or who felt better about themselves or who had greater peace of mind as a result of immorality" (*No Doubt About It* [2001], 194). The gospel standards are evidence of God's love for us, since they protect us from unhappy consequences. Just as every action has a reaction, every choice has a consequence.

THOU ART STILL CHOSEN

*But remember, God is merciful; therefore, repent of that which thou hast done which is contrary to the commandment which I gave you, and **thou art still chosen**, and art again called to the work.*

—D&C 3:10

WE ARE HUMAN, AND WE MESS THINGS UP, SOMETIMES DAILY. However, the sacrament table—the formal symbol of the Atonement—is never more than a week away, and our chosen status is not necessarily forfeited by sin. Even the Prophet of the Restoration made mistakes, as this scripture attests. Sister Julie B. Beck taught, "Sometimes people give up when they have made mistakes and come to believe that there is no hope for them. Some people imagine that they will feel better about themselves if they just leave the restored gospel and go away. It is Satan who puts hopeless thoughts in the hearts of those who have made mistakes. The Lord Jesus Christ always gives us hope" ("Remembering, Repenting, and Changing," *Ensign,* May 2007, 111). Aminadab's companions were floundering in the darkness when he encouraged them to exercise faith in Christ, "who was taught unto you by Alma, and Amulek, and Zeezrom" (Helaman 5:41)—three chosen missionaries, each of whom had an imperfect past.

CAN YE
LOOK UP?

*I say unto you, **can ye look up** to God at that day with a pure heart and clean hands? I say unto you, can you look up, having the image of God engraven upon your countenances?*

—Alma 5:19

ALMA COULD HAVE USED MANY DIFFERENT PHRASES TO MAKE HIS POINT. He could have asked, "Are you clean?" "Have you been forgiven?" or "Did you repent?" Instead, he asked a simple question: "Can ye look up?" Earlier in his life, Alma's soul was racked for three days and three nights as he contemplated coming into God's presence. Here he's asking his listeners to envision the same inevitable reunion, and to predict their own posture. When we are ashamed, when we've done something we know we shouldn't have done, our natural inclination is to look down, to shrivel, to bury our heads in our hands and try to shut out the memory. However, through the grace of Christ and with the glorious gift of repentance, we don't have to shrivel or hide or look down in shame and regret. While it is likely we will be kneeling at such a reunion with the Lord, we won't be afraid of eye contact. We can look up!

POWERFUL MESSAGES
IN FIVE WORDS

LET HIM ASK OF GOD

If any of you lack wisdom,
let him ask of God, *that giveth
to all men liberally, and upbraideth
not; and it shall be given him.*

—James 1:5

THESE FIVE WORDS IN THE EPISTLE OF JAMES CHANGED THE WORLD. Joseph Smith's first prayer is traceable to this verse of scripture and the powerful impression that it left on his soul. The consequences of that teenage prayer led many thousands to cross oceans and continents in an attempt to build Zion. But this verse was not written for Joseph Smith alone. The message of James 1:5 for the rest of us is that God is approachable, generous, and willing to answer our prayers. An additional implication is that if we don't ask of God, He won't give liberally. Later in the epistle, James writes, "Ye have not, because ye ask not" (James 4:2). In the same spirit, Elder Jeffrey R. Holland taught, "God is anxiously waiting for the chance to answer your prayers and fulfill your dreams, just as He always has. But He can't if you don't pray, and He can't if you don't dream. In short, He can't if you don't believe" (*Broken Things to Mend* [2008], 85).

HERE AM I,
SEND ME

*And the Lord said: Whom
shall I send? And one answered
like unto the Son of Man:*
Here am I, send me.

—Abraham 3:27

HOW CAN ONE DESCRIBE WHAT THESE FIVE WORDS HAVE MEANT to every son and daughter of God? Jesus Christ, the greatest of all, volunteered to descend below all things and to suffer beyond anything mortals could suffer, doing for us what we could not do for ourselves. Interestingly, Abraham and Moses used a similar phrase when the Lord called, but the prophet Isaiah used Jehovah's exact words, "Here am I; send me" (see Genesis 22:1; Exodus 3:4; Isaiah 6:8). All of us have the opportunity to choose our own words when we are issued difficult callings. How will we answer? Elder Dallin H. Oaks taught, "Please consider who it is you are refusing or neglecting to serve when you decline a calling or when you accept, promise, and fail to fulfill" ("I'll Go Where You Want Me to Go," *Ensign,* November 2002, 69). When we plead with our Heavenly Father to send us help as we attempt to magnify a new calling or respond to a new challenge, I believe the Savior responds once again, "Here am I, send me."

ART THOU GREATER THAN HE?

*The Son of Man hath
descended below them all.*
Art thou greater than he?

—D&C 122:8

SINCE OUR CHILDHOOD WE'VE BEEN TAUGHT THE "LAW OF RETRIBUTION": Do good, and be rewarded with good; do evil, and be rewarded with evil. And that is absolutely true. Sometimes. And sometimes it isn't. Indeed, it's possible to do the right thing and still suffer. Just ask Job, Joseph of Egypt, Abraham, Nephi, or Abinadi. Yet often, when we suffer, we might ask "why?"

None of us are so great that we can claim exemption from adversity. Elder Neal A. Maxwell observed, "He felt our very pains and afflictions before we did. . . . Since the most innocent one suffered the most, our own cries of 'why?' cannot match His" (*If Thou Endure It Well* [1996], 52). When we understand the fruits of suffering, we see that "all these things shall give [us] experience, and shall be for [our] good" (D&C 122:7). Ultimately, in the final judgment, the law of retribution will apply. But in this life, for divine purposes often unknown to us, we will have tribulation. The greatest among us may suffer greatly.

LABORING WITH THEIR OWN HANDS

Every man should esteem his neighbor as himself, **laboring with their own hands** *for their support.*

—Mosiah 27:4

WHAT WE OFTEN CALL THE "WORK ETHIC" WAS INSTITUTED IN THE GARDEN OF EDEN. Our first parents were told, "In the sweat of thy face shalt thou eat bread" (Genesis 3:19). Notice, it is by the sweat of *thy* face, the Lord said, not by the sweat of others' faces that we should eat. And under King Mosiah, the people labored with their *own* hands for their support, not expecting others' hands to work for them. Following the death of Lehi in the New World, Nephi was warned to take his followers and leave the land of their first inheritance. And what did Nephi teach his people once they settled in their new home? "I, Nephi, did cause my people to be industrious, and to labor with their hands" (2 Nephi 5:17). Working, and working for our own support when we are capable, is a principle of the gospel. President Ezra Taft Benson warned, "[You] have heard some express that it is their right to be supported by another man's labor. That philosophy is wrong. It has proved the ruination of character in individuals and the downfall of nations" (*LDS Church News,* September 4, 1993).

THE DAY OF THIS LIFE

*For behold, this life is the time for men to prepare to meet God; yea, behold **the day of this life** is the day for men to perform their labors.*

—Alma 34:32

PERHAPS ONLY ONE WITH AN ETERNAL PERSPEC-
TIVE COULD REFER TO A LIFETIME AS A "DAY."
In the next verse, Amulek continues his discourse
against procrastination, "after *this day of life,* which
is given us to prepare for eternity, behold, if we do
not improve our time while in this life, then cometh
the night of darkness wherein there can be no labor
performed" (Alma 34:33; emphasis added). "This
day of life," but what a day! What a difference a day
makes. President Henry B. Eyring observed: "There
is a danger in the word *someday* when what it means
is 'not this day.' 'Someday I will repent.' 'Someday I
will forgive him.' 'Someday I will speak to my friend
about the Church.' 'Someday I will start to pay tith-
ing.' 'Someday I will return to the temple.'" President
Eyring continued, "We will weep, and [God] will
weep, if we have intended to repent and to serve Him
in tomorrows which never came or have dreamt of
yesterdays where the opportunity to act was past. This
day is a precious gift of God" ("This Day," *Ensign,*
May 2007, 89).

ARE WE NOT ALL BEGGARS?

For behold, **are we not all beggars?**

—Mosiah 4:19

KING BENJAMIN'S SPEECH IS A TREASURE, AND THIS PHRASE IS ONE OF ITS GEMS. In only five words, King Benjamin confronts the idea of "works righteousness," or of salvation by works alone, by asking, "Are we not all beggars?" Not one of us can approach the Lord and demand eternal life based on our own merits. We simply don't have what it takes. When it comes to our salvation, we cannot earn it or demand it. The Golden Rule teaches that we should do unto others as we would have them do unto us. But King Benjamin admonishes his listeners to do more—to do unto others as *God* has done unto them, to be merciful and impart of their substance one to another, just as God has been merciful and imparted salvation to us. Thus, our works are necessary, but not sufficient. Our righteous works are fruits of the Spirit; they are a result, not a cause, of our being forgiven and converted to Christ. Our works will assist us in becoming what the Lord wants us to become, but, as Moroni taught, we must rely "alone upon the merits of Christ, who [is] the author and the finisher of [our] faith" (Moroni 6:4).

PURE HEARTS
AND CLEAN
HANDS

*Believe in Christ,
and worship the Father in
his name, with **pure hearts
and clean hands**.*

—2 Nephi 25:16

THE ANCIENTS OFTEN USED BODY PARTS TO DESCRIBE MANKIND'S SPIRITUAL CONDITION. The Psalmist asked, "Who shall ascend into the hill of the Lord? or who shall stand in his holy place?" (dual references to the temple). The answer is given, "He that hath clean hands, and a pure heart" (Psalm 24:3–4; see also Alma 5:19). Interestingly, the phrase *clean hands and a pure heart* is another way of describing "justification and sanctification." To be justified is to have clean hands, or to be pronounced clean from sin. To be sanctified is to have a pure heart, or to have lost the desire to sin. Someone who says, "I'll sin now and repent later," believes that repentance can clean his or her hands but obviously does not possess a pure heart. The gift of the Atonement provides the opportunity for both justification and sanctification by not only cleansing our hands from past sins but also purifying our hearts and helping us lose desire for sin.

GREAT PRIVILEGE OF OUR CHURCH

*Therefore, my beloved brother, Moroni, let us resist evil, and whatsoever evil we cannot resist with our words, yea, such as rebellions and dissensions, let us resist them with our swords, that we may retain our freedom, that we may rejoice in the **great privilege of our church**, and in the cause of our Redeemer and our God.*

—Alma 61:14

IN OUR MODERN DAY, MANY HAVE BECOME CRITICAL OF ANY TYPE OF ORGANIZED RELIGION. One of the more popular sayings recently is, "Well, I'm spiritual, but not religious." Some believe in Jesus, but suggest that He didn't intend to organize a church, He only sought to articulate a set of beliefs. But the fact is, He *did* organize a church. Not only has the gospel of Jesus Christ been restored, but the Church—the organization that administers His gospel—is restored as well. The Church of Jesus Christ is the kingdom of God on earth, which not only encourages but equips its members to learn, grow, and become. The Church is the organization where the keys are housed, where the ordinances are obtained, and where the priesthood lives. Some will say, "I know the gospel is true," but hesitate to say "the Church is true," because it is filled to the brim with imperfect people. But that is exactly what God intended: that we would learn to grow toward perfection in the midst of imperfection. For these reasons, we rejoice in the great privilege of our church.

THAT I MAY HEAL YOU

O all ye that are spared because ye were more righteous than they, will ye not now return unto me, and repent of your sins, and be converted, **that I may heal you**?

—3 Nephi 9:13

WHAT OLD TESTAMENT VERSE BEST DE-SCRIBES THE SAVIOR'S ROLE? Actually, we don't have to wonder, or research, or rely on the work of scholars, because the Savior Himself answered the question when He announced His ministry. Returning to a synagogue in Nazareth, and choosing a scroll of Esaias (or Isaiah), He proclaimed, "The Spirit of the Lord is upon me, because he hath anointed me to preach the gospel to the poor; he hath sent me to heal the brokenhearted, to preach deliverance to the captives, and recovering of sight to the blind, to set at liberty them that are bruised." Then He sat down and announced, "This day is this scripture fulfilled in your ears" (Luke 4:17–21). The Savior could have chosen any verse from the entire Torah that day, but He chose to speak of Himself as a healer of hearts. President Marion G. Romney taught that someone may know he is converted "when by the power of the Holy Spirit his soul is healed" (in Conference Report, October 1963, 25).

ABOUT THE AUTHOR

John Bytheway served a mission to the Philippines and later graduated from Brigham Young University. A favorite speaker and teacher, John holds a master's degree in Religious Education and is a part-time instructor at BYU. John is the author of many bestselling books, audio talks, and DVDs, including three scripture commentaries: *Of Pigs, Pearls, and Prodigals: A Fresh Look at the Parables of Jesus; Isaiah for Airheads;* and *Righteous Warriors: Lessons from the War Chapters in the Book of Mormon.* He and his wife, Kimberly, have six children.